Yoga Poetry

POSE POEMS TO ENHANCE YOUR PRACTICE

samantha Lang

Foreword by Cheryl Oliver

Yoga Poetry

© 2015 Samantha Lang

Photography: Joe Irvine

Models: Mycal Anders, Candace Cotton, Roxanne Frederick, Matthew Hodges, Samantha Lang, David Seamans, Michael Shumsky, Stephanie Yager, and Kristina Zozuls

DEDICATION

For my mother, Sheila Vandercar Lang.

CONTENTS

FOREWORD

It is my pleasure to write a few words here to introduce Samantha Lang and her work, Yoga Poetry: Pose Poems to Enhance Your Practice. My late husband Dave Oliver and I met Samantha when she was in the yoga teacher training Dave taught at At One Yoga in Scottsdale, Arizona in the summer of 2004, and she quickly became not only our student, but also our friend.

That teacher training was a four-week summer intensive and over long days filled with asana, practice teaching, and learning Sanskrit, the group bonded through intense, shared experiences including inversion practice immediately after lunch, fondly christened "vomit-asana." Many of us remain friends to this day, more than ten years after the training ended.

The volume you hold in your hands pays homage to one of the oldest precepts of yoga, that while it is true we learn through our own experience, those who have trod the path before us can help us along our way by relating their experience via eloquent language, and what is "eloquent language," if not poetry?

The veda, the foundational texts of yoga philosophy, are all written in poetic meter. The wisdom of the veda was considered to be too important for ordinary speech. Hence, meter ("chandas" in Sanskrit) elevates words ("śabda") which together have the ability to reveal hidden meaning, to reveal truth.

When we approach the veda, we can follow a cyclical process of words ("yajñika"), stories ("itihāsa"), and inspiration ("parivrājaka"). We start with the words, which are explained in the stories, which then evoke the feelings, which inspire us and so in turn give voice to the words. The process continues on and on through subsequent layers of understanding.

Each poem in this book conveys "...a philosophical meditation on the experience of being in the posture," as Samantha Lang writes in her Introduction, and so this is not an instruction manual; it is much, much more. By elevating her words with meter, Samantha has tapped into arguably the most profound way to convey the mystery of human experience.

She has connected with the ancient lineage of the veda and, like the sages of old, she relates her experience in eloquent language. She offers words and stories of her experience which elicit in the reader myriad feelings, which then inspire us to return to the words again and again to reveal deeper layers of meaning.

The best teachers know they cannot have the experience for you. Having had their own experience, the teacher is always there to lovingly guide you on your journey and to support you through your experience, even if they "don't like to talk" (Good Teacher, page 38).

We are fortunate that Samantha Lang likes to write and we are grateful for her gift of Yoga Poetry to guide us as we each progress on our path.

Cheryl Oliver
Scottsdale, Arizona
September, 2015

INTRODUCTION

"You see, yoga is an immensely expressive figurative poetry that, when captured in the right light, it shows humanity's longing to reach our full potential."

—Robert Sturman, Photographer (*"Yoga Meets Art — Create a Life You Love,"* Rebelle Society, August 2014)

This book unites two personal passions -- yoga and poetry. Having composed my first poem at the age of three (my mother wrote it down for me), my roots in writing span every decade of my life. Not until my twenties, however, did I enter my first yoga posture. After a good deal of physical practice, I realized; this is sacred poetry spoken through the body. Something very wise is singing its ancient song through the human form.

Yet, yoga can be elusive. Transformative, meditative practices can be overturned by a sudden injury, a heavy day when the body won't cooperate, too much energy or too little, an overactive mind, the judging ego. This list is long. But over time, we learn to bow to the power of the tradition and go with what is, knowing we're just seekers -- of the countless -- walking its well-worn path. We're not going to push this rock uphill by sheer acts of will. No, we are at its beautiful mercy.

The same holds true in the creative writing realm. One can possess years of training in the craft, but still can't force a poem into being. It will only reveal itself by allowing it to do so in its own way. Poets listen to sound and meaning with acute awareness so that we may capture lovely flutterings of language. The words may fly away. Poetry is a delicate art of tuning oneself to verbal beauty and learning how to capture it eventually, gently in the net of concentrated phrases and sentences.

It is with great reverence for the traditions of yoga and poetry that I submit this homage to both. The poems intend to convey a philosophical meditation on the experience of being in the posture. They are not meant to accurately explain historical meaning. I'll leave that to the Sanskrit scholars. Instead, these poems are personal, my own discoveries of what they can mean.

The photographs are meant to provide visual support to explore the meaning of the poems. If you look deeply at each photo, you may feel the energy of the posture. Apply that energy to the reading and see what is revealed.

I hope this book brings you pleasure. If you are a yogi, may it enhance your practice. If you've never set foot on a yoga mat, may it transfer to you the joy of being there.

Namaste,
Samantha Lang

1

ACKNOWLEDGEMENTS

I offer deep thanks to those who have enriched my understanding and love of yoga. I am permanently grateful to have received the teachings of Dave and Cheryl Oliver. Thank you also to John Salisbury, Ian Lopatin, Aaron King, David Romanelli, and Bear Tobin.

My poetry owes much to Henry Taylor, my graduate school professor and mentor at American University. My thanks to you are beyond words and should have been expressed years ago.

To the great minds whose work continually informs the way I perceive the world, I extend eternal gratitude to Jalaluddin Rumi, Coleman Barks, The Tao te Ching, Stephen Mitchell, Deepak Chopra, Wayne Dyer, Eckhart Tolle, Carolyn Myss, Thich Nhat Hanh, Christiane Northrup, and Sri Swami Satchidananda.

Tremendous thanks for all of the unconditional love Mom, Dad, Debbie, Graham, Billy, Jim, Andrew, Patricia, Candace, Megan, Stephanie, SD, Trent, Jennifer and many other friends along the way. I love you.

Vritti Haiku

The non-stop onslaught
of perpetual thought talks
you out of changing.

~~~

Still, the soul Self shows
a good road ahead: inside
yoga, the True you.

Balasana — Child's Pose

Here we begin again.
There's been no pain,
no assault yet against
your spirit. You know
no tumult, no shame, no
reason to cover your back
or your fat, laughing belly.
Heart, head, and hands rest
on Earth and you trust Her
completely to feed and treat
you as sweetly as a mother.
Your past is so small; it barely
exists. Only your large future
bursts from this Nowness, rich
with wisdom traditions rolling
out their mystic roads. Whichever
way you go is The Way if you learn
well to unlearn, reset, and return
to the wide-minded awe of a child.

Padahastasana — Foot to Hand Pose

Today my attention fell open
like a bag of glass marbles.
My mind rolled wildly like two
hundred separate spheres.
I had to contain myself, rein
my brain from chasing small,
childish, sparkly things. So I bent
and buried ten busy fingers under
bare and burdened heels. I began
to breathe as if through the roof
of my head until the circuit lit,
the sweet, eternal current of being.
Thought dimmed and a crisp clarity
rose within the space of the sacred
connection. Soles can read palms.
Listen to what the inner teller says.

Trikonasana — Triangle Pose

Stretch in the three directions
but never leave the center. A higher
future at your fingertips, the past
behind but guiding, yet everything
depends on the present, the primary
quality of energy you emit. Certain
days the body conveys messages
like a courier. Other times, the mind
sells wild rides, so you buckle down
and go. Soul moments you know
as openings, sudden proficiency
with sacred geometry. See cleverly
nested shapes, so-called negative
space between the thighs, its peak
the portal for every mortal. Tap
the potential to untangle puzzling
angles, proofs of acute hurt. Study
equally strength, balance, flexibility
— shanti in the wisdom of trinities.

Utthita Parsvakonasana —
Extended Side Angle Pose

Outline the story of your body.
These lines spell out your interior
dialogue, reveal years of beliefs,
and speak volumes on how you think
you should appear. Today, a new page
flashes in the palm of your extended
hand. Only you can read that future.
The posture says reach further; the next
chapter uncovers more meaning, character
developed by dismissing stress and the mix
of toxic mindsets, studying the underlying
bliss inside a slow exhale. Inhale the will
to be a work in progress, a perfect disaster
of a masterpiece perpetually revising itself.
We all have an angle, a point of view, but
never stop asking why. Freely recreate,
define anew, the latest version of you.

Prasarita Padottanasa E — Expanded Foot Pose

This is how you'll grow more
true in all you do. Grab ahold
of your outer edges and dive in.
What you perceive as limitation
is merely expectation, thinking
you know where you stand. Inner
expansion goes beyond the length
of space you take. Spirit, the pure
search for purpose brought you here
to learn the worth of an open heart,
valiant when vulnerable. Universal
law rewards courage with more courage,
and forward folding hastens change,
so keep bending deeply into yourself,
even if difficult. Trust that just as
you will soon unfold and stand, so will
the master plan; the God-illuminated
future stretches out in front of you.

Hanumanasana — Monkey Pose

I'll go over oceans to show you
what yoga can do. The pose of pure
devotion blows Energy's front door
wide open. Walk inside. She'll feed
you more of what makes Her. There
you'll taste a fullness that never fades.
I've reached a sustained state of belief
in leaps of faith, in quantum expansion.
It's possible to dissolve every obstacle
with love if we avoid being hamstrung
by appointed outcomes. Watch in awe
after offering mountainous generosity
of spirit. You'll split your concept of limits
to bits. Explode old perceptions and fly
over fields of possibility. Stretch beyond
the strain of dedication to attain the bliss
of worship. Lose and find yourself in service.

Vriksasana — Tree Pose

Before I knew I was choosing
everything, before I could see
the wishing tree inside me,
I misperceived the outside world
as outside. Now, no wind blows
that's not my own making in some way.
Today, I pray in the space of *ananda
kanda. Ananda hum*, the mantra
I repeat means to reach the roots
of bliss, to grow it from deep within,
through trunk to limb to leaf, to seed
the world with what it needs. Peace
within is peace unbroken. I plant a wish
beneath my heart. May it spread
evergreen in the center above
and fuel forever the wheel of love.

Virabadrasana — Warrior Pose

Behind me is what I know,
before me, the strength
to change. Grounded here,
I fear no future matter, aligned
at the center with an infinite
source of power. No need
to look back; I feel my inner
rudder cutting the water of all
I've ever learned. What I choose
to see is shaped by the eyes
of the warrior inside. Clarity first,
then action. I'm ready to be equally
at ease in the heat of battle as I am
in peaceful leisure. I can rest here
in the posture of confidence. Pure,
without violence, without a shield
across my chest, I face whatever
comes next with potent openness.

Virabadrasana 2 — Warrior 2 Pose

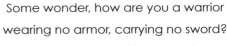

Some wonder, how are you a warrior
wearing no armor, carrying no sword?
The metal made of inner mastery
protects me, the blade of experience
with ways of other worlds shines ready
at my side. Ordeals of crossing ego's
minefields, forging humble passage
dressed in dirt, ignoring culture's voice
urging me back to high ground and losing
all trust in sight and sound, I trained myself
to walk away from words of praise, to leave
diamonds in the mud for the next seeker
on the road. My feet tread deeper realms
of battle, holy war with my own fear. Here,
after years, I can enter the pose of heart
and blindside exposure, exhibit the vital
stance of knowing the privilege of living
free of worry, weaponless in an armed world.

Virabadrasana 3 — Warrior 3 Pose

If private pain processed you
to be who you do not dream
of being, let love undo that.
A warrior on a wobbly leg
still stands. Expose your chest
to Earth and ask Her to infuse
you with heart strength. Watch
yourself from afar and affirm
you are an observer blessed
with a gift for decrypting symbols
all around. Perhaps right under
your nose lie the codes to transmute
worry into wisdom, hell into health,
poverty to wealth. An inner heaven
beams in every being, but seeing
is not believing. Close your eyes
to feel your body lifted by the sky.
Elevate to your spirit's natural state.

Bakasana — Crane Pose

Believe in self-healing. Swallow
the mental pill of how you want
to feel. You are your own placebo.
There's no telling how high you'll fly
by whispering yes to weightlessness.
Go ahead and push the floor away;
hover over lower places. Like a bird,
your body readily lands, but with the lift
of flight. Transcend your troubles as if
they weren't your own. The distance
lets you see spaces awaiting your next
move. What you thought impossible
was just a blocked eye's view. The pose
says shift to a daring new perspective.
Straight-arm the ground to enter the air.
Free your head to get better up there.

Paschimottanasana —
Intense West-body Stretch

My tense personal self says sorry
to my spirit self. I'm so imperfect.
I've paved my way with mistakes.
Go west, young yogi, the forgiving
spirit replies. Keep trying. Explore
the back side of your body, vulnerable
as skin. If you wish to suffer less,
bend further into the unseen. Pain
evaporates when you concentrate
on present breath. Every hour now
perceive yourself as a pioneer never
quite reaching the coast. The joy is
in the traveling not arriving. There
is no perfect person, only seekers
with curious hands and feet. How do
you know you're worthy of carrying on,
continuing to reach forward? You are
alive and here to seek the source
of light emblazoning your eyes.

Tadasana — Mountain Pose

The mind of the mountain maintains
itself with wholeness. What goes up
may not come down; this oneness
knows no opposites. Here, there is
nowhere to go. The pose unmoved
by excuses dismisses resistance
to stillness and calls all wandering
back to the path. Let climbers come
and claim to surmount its surface,
pride displacing prayer. Beware of those
who never bow and kiss the ground,
crouched in the delusion of power over
nature. Deep crevices, cleaving of ideas,
raw sierras, these peaks are not problems
to overcome, but answers hung on the wall
of the sky. Stand firm in the truth of who
you are, both low and highlands, temporal
and eternal, now a person, always a soul.

Garudasana — Eagle Pose

Wring into your limbs for fuel to light
the spinal fuse. Time to neutralize
your poisons, however consumed,
through people, places, mouth or
mind. Your burdens will burn when
this God-bird extends its wingspan,
wide and fiery, capable of scorching
the sun. No venom survives the pose
that devours inner demons. Submit
to its difficulty. Its twisted contradictions
subside when you go inside and find
what's fighting. Whatever bites, hisses
or coils, call it up with gentleness, then
say a kind goodbye. The eagle eye locks
on what you need gone, swooping down
to doom the shadows that weaken you.

Natarajasana — Lord of the Dance Pose

The skills masters build through lives
of practice, felt in every cell, we call
awareness. Greats express this depth
of access with exotic body shapes,
creating choreographed creatures
that leap from the unmanifest into clear
view. But what really dances before you
can't be seen, only gleaned with attuned
intuition. Watch a guru reach behind
his back into a shadowy bag of tricks.
It's not his hands you'll feel as you leave
the ground. Grace is power, authentic
as a river, and neither thought nor might
will stop it. As currents flow over rocks,
the fluid movers smooth and overcome
the fixed ones. Look more closely if you
think a pose motionless. Or tell a dancer
to stand still. Even that will be a dance.

Ahdo Mukha Vrksasana — Downward Facing Tree Pose

Don't think about it! Just feel
the flush of freedom, the rush
of blood and pulse countered by
breath control. It's in your hands,
this moment, to seize just as
a mischievous breeze grabs
the tree leaves and shakes
them silly. Play with your world
this way. Kick up your heels,
cartwheel, and fall. It's all okay
if you keep your chin and vibe
up, and finally face down this limb
of truth: there is absolutely nothing
to fear. So be here, enlightened
if only for moments. All is aligned
and well, even while the whole
wild world turns upside down.

Ardha Chandrasana — Half Moon Pose

You come from the cosmos
and contain the universe just
as it does you. We are not free
of one another, rather droplets
equaling the sea. The secret-
keepers speak to you in sleep.
You're a system within a system
within a mystery. Be a natural
satellite to your source planet,
locked in worship with your bliss.
Imagine the Earth-smitten moon,
whose love-orbit pulls tides of brine
and blood far outside her sphere,
her circling reaffirming the breathing
union of expansion and contraction.
Your energy too extends beyond
gravity. If night seems to be the only
sea you swim, shine on. Your light
no doubt breaks someone's dark apart.

Pincha Mayurasana — Peacock Feather Pose

I could woo you with my beauty.
But I will not do it. This display
of grace is staged by the play
of nature. All danger disarms itself
in my presence. I make snakes
uncoil. Dancing cooly along the cliff,
it's the mountain that reconsiders
its position, while my feathers fly wildly
blessing earth and sky. I'd pin your eyes
wide open with tales of swimming jeweled
pools of endless possibility. The miraculous
takes practice though, so I forearm myself
daily with postures of poise and peace
and breathing fear away. Suspended
inverted in space, myself an act of magic
iridescence, I can shoulder this and any
difficulty. Truly, all is coming, perfectly.

Virasana — Hero Pose

I have been weak. Formerly,
my ego screamed needs
I held people to meet. Not me
then, the cause was always you.
Fight me until my sheer virility
shrinks you. Bow down and make
me big. But now, after years in
the humble steadiness of practice,
I am strong, one with emptiness,
one with all. Facing flattery or insult,
I feel the same, unshaken; my old mind
rests in ashes. Brave and kneeling,
feeling a boundless universe
urgently requesting I rise. I can
lead the way by being the living
victory of peace and smallness.

Ustrasana — Camel Pose (Variation)

I have been blown back,
blasted in the heart by the bad
behavior of others, the glue-eyed
thieves of peace, hard, hunched
squatters soiling sacred ground.
But that is not for me now to plot
out what to do. That is not for me.
For me, clear speech and honesty
to finally drain past poisons trapped
in the thought-body. Change each
assailant's name just to "sufferer." Aim
to serve, to ease their hurt as fervently
as my own. I trust my own dark weight
will one day lift and tears will stream
from me, not from a sad, scarred heart,
but one grown open and set free.

Kapotasana — Pigeon Pose

I'd rather make the shape of it
than say it. Maybe it's too complex
to be said. Yoga lovers discover
heart trumps head. It's best I not
serve you words but rather curves:
a waist that awaits your fingers to find
its underside. I can bend your mind
like the spine of a leaf with flourished
inflection and crystalline wit, but now
is not the time. By my side, upside
down, you spin my inner compass
around. This pigeon can't find home
without the sound of your breath
next to mine. Let's practice good old-
fashioned human union until those poses
know our names. This laughing path
to happiness started where soul worlds
met. Let's pack our bags and get back.
I built an arc to light the long way home.

Rajakapotasana — King Pigeon Pose

How are you royal and still humble?
Don't you see the neighbors shake
their heads when you take the hand
of the hunched man to thank him
for planting bright flowers outside
your great house gates? They think
you pay him too much attention, yet
your kingdom expands more quickly
than you can give away your money.
It's said you beat the ego clean out
of your head with the sole of your own
dirty foot. It took years to find comfort
in the noble pose, chest boldly exposed,
legs split, rooting yet kicking. At last, you
rest in your magnificence, diminished
by no one. Greatness takes all under
its wing, warming the world heart
with unapologetic self-expression.

Setu Bandhasana — Bridge Pose (Variation)

Bridge the distance between anger and forgiveness. Each resistance requires inspection, tapping at the old scaffolding of thinking. Link by introspection the mental architecture of failure to the wisdom it permitted. Waves hit and shook the structure, but your footing held firm. Slack wanderers squandered your offer to cross them over churning water, but this didn't end your generous bending. You sensed the blessings of posing as a passage, pondering yoga, bonding body and soul, the transient to the permanent. Arching, you mimic the firmament, a luminous fusion of earth and the eternal curve of heaven.

Urdva Danurasana — Upward Bow Pose

When I enter my heart, there
You are. The reminder of how
to find Her, best self, the cure
for complacence, the fire-starter
of greater hunger and passion,
the backbend remodels the body
into a hollow bow awaiting an arrow.
Focus and shoot for more verdure
from chakra four. Allow intention
to take aim that I may earn true
change from pain, that I learn
to seek purity out of adversity,
and joy even in suffering, feeling
incessantly the energy of the one
center none can live without. I set
the target that even at my worst,
when pressed, stressed, stretched,
or hurt, I can rise above and tender
solely sure, broad-shouldered love.

Baddha Konasana —
Bound Angle Pose

The separation illusion fades.
We dissolve into the God-water
of unity consciousness. Like fingers
and toes woven together, we are one
body recycling global blood, a shared
liquid and airstream. We live together,
breathe each other, knowing there is
no *other*, only eras of cells in skulls
evolving billions of bodily boundaries.
What if we could grasp the concept
of difference without tightening
our grip? What if we could relax
into contrast and see our walking
in another set of feet? The angle
and angst of limbs limit how deeply
we dive in, but let's swim the infinite
network until we remember, being is
boundless; only the mind contains us.

Salamba Sarvangasana —
Supported Shoulderstand

My head works better after
I stand next to it for a bit. Clunky
thinker out of the picture, I'll hang
here until every cell turns clear.
I can transform myself. Stillness
is a myth, as big a trick as solidity.
I've watched meditation change me
from body to no-body to the now-body
in The One. Most times it's just fine
to surf brain waves, gamma space
from the peace place: the prefrontal
sea of cortex, where time does not exist.
I've conditioned my body to broker
prayer, but the strength to support
this entire structure comes from where
my simple mind will never enter.

Halasana — Plow Pose

Ready the ground above your head
for seeds. Your brightest dreams
begin here. They will take root
and appear by learning to steer
the ancient mind-body machine. Turn
the upper layers of soil and soul
will surface, infinite nutrient to fuel
the growth of fields. Be easily drawn,
well-oiled, and sharp enough to break
the creep of weeds that can corrupt
your land. Cut the remains of past
crops, barren or bountiful. It's time
to tend to Now. Tilling row after row
of pure potential, the patient plow
does not plant nor sow. It prepares.
It trusts; the next harvest will be best.

Karnapidasana — Ear Pressure Pose

When the world is loud, when your head
kicks at its cage, when you need to untie
entanglements between your hips,
or forgive actions trapped in your lower
back, place both knees over your ears
in a thigh-high recline. Hum hush
to the chattering skull ball until it is dark
and sparkless. A sparkly marble will find
you trouble. You'll tell your lover you want
another. You'll think in terms of better
and have too much to say. Stop before
you reason reason's reasons all day.
Sometimes you just need to squeeze
your head with your knees and breathe.

33

Sirsasana — Headstand

Drain the doubt out. Your purpose
lives with your bliss. Once you toss
the blockage of being a fallen being,
you'll see worry stories for what they are –
made-up mind stuff. Fear rules the uptight,
the upright, not you. Don't beg angels
to your shoulders. Shake the fantasy
and wake to not needing wings. Divinity
lives within. Your essence once opted
to leave the unseen and become form
in your mother's womb. We go Home soon
through Earth's sweet dirt, but until then,
let's stand on the stars. They're ours,
angels, to tiptoe like stones in a river.
From here, the path ahead looks clear:
dive headlong wherever your spirit leads.

Yoga Mudra — Seal of the Yogi

Am I bound by my body
to be tied down to human
suffering? Why, when the rising
feeling keeps coming. Oneness
weaves me into we repeatedly.
Transcending duality: yoga is real,
the flaring ego a dream. This whole
body seal reveals great figure eights;
hands and feet stitch the rings of infinity.
My family is humanity but my home
is not here. The inner core expands
and demands union with a spaceless
space, a *there* where all souls assemble.
Now, in our small skins, we can at least
bow to each day, to the grace to give
hope to raise the hate cultures, to stay
inspired and pray for an age of peace.

Padmasana — Lotus Pose

The difficulty begins in the simple,
physical resistances. The hips
with their victim stories storing
stiffness in the joints. Angry ankles
argue and the knees bark back. But,
somewhere in there lives an original
openness. Like a flower, our miracle
is to be fragile, delicate as fragrance.
Yet we forget and get heavy, stuck in
mud and dead set on sinking. Enter
the transcendent pose. It will save you,
connecting form to formlessness. Submit
as its thin ribbons lift the body to float over
whatever dirty water plagues. We discover
space in which to hover above ugliness,
remaining untainted. What things of beauty,
we who practice the lotus, who take our
seats alone, in stillness making waves.

Savasana — Corpse Pose

An hour ago, you were a child.
You entered this world screamingly
alive, pure light behind your eyes,
and grew to prove true the biological
miracle of the physical. Perpetually
regenerating, you witnessed mysterious
disappearances of former selves. Yoga
cleared the course for countless little
practice lifetimes: balasana to savasana,
teaching strength to weakness, release
to constraint, the peace of least resistance.
This rest refreshes energies just spent, drains
the unnecessary. Nearly breathless, blessing
death, you can kiss your biggest fear goodnight.
The pose of repose says no more composing
songs of pranayama, close the channels of eyes
and mind. Leave life as you know it behind.

Good Teacher
—for Dave Oliver

I said to the guru, "Please tell all
you know to me, so that I can grow
into your nature and your strength.

Please let me wake at the foot
of your low bed, bowing to shadow
you through daytime. Let me witness

your mystic madness through even
one night." The teacher grinned,
"I don't like to talk." I followed,

"Let me listen to that, then."

Yoga High Haiku

All is well. Mindstorms,

qualms, all worries gone to calm.

Here is where we are.

ABOUT SAMANTHA LANG

Samantha Lang is an avid yoga practitioner and instructor in Phoenix and Scottsdale, Arizona. Certified in 2004 by At One Yoga, Samantha was trained by Astanga yoga master, Dave Oliver, and Sanskrit scholar, Cheryl Hall Oliver. Samantha holds a BA in English from Fordham University and an MFA in Creative Writing from American University.

Follow, friend, and find Samantha:

- www.yogaandpoetry.com

- Twitter: @samanthalang

- Facebook: www.facebook.com/yogapoetry

- Instagram: yogapoetry_thebook